Alexis Bloomer

ARCHWAY
PUBLISHING

Archway Publishing books may be ordered through booksellers or by contacting:

Archway Publishing
1663 Liberty Drive
Bloomington, IN 47403
www.archwaypublishing.com
1 (888) 242-5904

Because of the dynamic nature of the Internet, any web addresses or
links contained in this book may have changed since publication and
may no longer be valid. The views expressed in this work are solely those
of the author and do not necessarily reflect the views of the publisher,
and the publisher hereby disclaims any responsibility for them.

Any people depicted in stock imagery provided by Thinkstock are models,
and such images are being used for illustrative purposes only.
Certain stock imagery © Thinkstock.

ISBN: 978-1-4808-5328-7 (sc)
ISBN: 978-1-4808-5329-4 (hc)
ISBN: 978-1-4808-5330-0 (e)

Library of Congress Control Number: 2017916514

Print information available on the last page.

Archway Publishing rev. date: 11/7/2017

Contents

Introduction

If you're reading this book, I want to warn you that I'm not going to be politically correct; in fact, I'm going to be brutally honest. I didn't write this book to offend anyone. I wrote it to shine light on the issues that young women face every day. I'm twenty-three years old, and society has told me that to fit in I have to be like everyone else. I have made mistakes; by no means am I looking down on people who have made some of the mistakes mentioned in this book. I'm hoping that by touching on certain issues we can create a movement to incorporate elegance back into the female sex. I'm not like everyone else. I feel as if I stand out, and every girl who is passionate and confident will feel the same way. Thankfully my mom raised me to be a lady, and I still reflect that in my everyday attitude. I surround myself with a circle of women who also believe that morals are still mandatory and class is still expected. I love those types of women; I love women who embrace being different.

I may be considered different from the normal girl, but being different is not a bad thing, especially in today's society. Be different by being yourself—there is only one you. I'm not saying you should be different by dyeing your hair some crazy color or posting offensive pictures on social media. I'm suggesting you embrace the beauty that makes you one of a kind. When you are yourself, in your raw form, you are different. Different is cool. Being you is cool. If you take anything from this book, I hope that it is that—even though it is difficult—it is possible to be a good girl in a world that tells you that the bigger the your butt is the smaller your heart can be.

Dear Kind Girl,

You may be pretty and you may be talented, but no one will remember you if you're mean.

Is it not ironic that all the smart, sassy, and kind girls are the ones that have fairy tales written about them? Think about it. Cinderella had two evil stepsisters who treated her poorly, and the prince still chose her. Or take Belle, who befriended a beast. She saw the beauty that was on the inside rather than shunning him as the rest of her society had done before her. The point is that kindness is not weakness. Hatefulness is a weak persons imitation of strength. I would much rather be the girl who has the story written about her than the one who hurts others to make herself feel better. I am not saying that all you will find is love; through kindness you'll find success, too.

Let me take you back to high school. I was the cheerleading captain, homecoming queen, Miss SHS, class favorite, and—wait for it—I had very few friends. Don't get me wrong; I had friends, but there are none I still talk to. My freshman year I was bullied to the point that I started to think I was the problem. I was teased, mocked, and threatened through the Internet, and much more. Then a senior said something to me that I have never forgotten: "You aren't the problem—society is." Do you want to know the best part? Most of the girls who picked on me in high school are the same girls now asking me to write them letters of recommendation, help them land internships, or give them advice on how to be successful in their fields. How is that for irony?

However, I don't use that against them. Instead, I give them my best advice: "Be good to people, because you never know when you will need that person later or how he or she could shape you at that moment." Girls ask me all the time how I became successful at such a young age. It is honestly because, along with my work ethic, I have always taken the time to make people feel important. Kindness is the most valuable currency you have. Your ability to spread kindness in an unkind world is an attribute of strength. Several of you are probably thinking, *I've been kind, but I don't know why people are still being hateful.*

Basically, mean people are mean because they have been hurt or are insecure. *Bam!* Mystery solved.

I don't know about you, but I've always been the girl who wants to be a hero, not a victim. People who are mean are essentially playing victim. Some of them take on this role their whole life. *Do not play victim.* You're a victor, meant for so much more than hatefulness can offer you. When you are mean to someone because you have been hurt, you are mass producing the very issue that destroyed you. Don't pass on that trait! Instead, laugh it off. This doesn't mean you're a wimp or not standing up for yourself. It simply means you're not giving the problem your time. You cannot argue with ignorance, and you cannot educate it. In essence, it's all about how you want to be perceived. What do you want your legacy to be? Don't let your legacy be a bitter saga. Instead, be the girl who becomes a queen and builds an empire with the bricks that were thrown at her.

Many of you see me through my Instagram posts, tweets, or whatever I post on some form of social media. Everything I post is authentic. I'm extremely happy, but how could I not be? It would be easy to be discouraged by the girls who give me dirty looks in public or who sit near me and whisper about me. Honestly, that is just their own insecurities and has nothing to do with me. One thing I have learned is that being physically pretty doesn't necessarily make you a pretty person. Someone very close to me always tells me that my heart is what made him fall in love with me. I find that to be the biggest compliment I could receive.

So, if you are out in public, and someone (who probably is not making the best choices or representing him/herself in the best possible way) gives you a dirty look, smile. That person needs some sunshine in his/her angry life. You are beautiful, talented, and blessed with something God chose to give *only you.* That alone makes you worth being kind to.

Kind Girl's Things to Remember

- I vow to be the hero of my own story and not allow others' words or actions to steal my joy.
- I vow to practice kindness every day, even in the most bitter of times.
- I vow to not adopt the "mean-girls" behavior that is present around me.
- I vow to take the high road.
- I vow to be beautiful on the inside.

Dear Social Girl,

You can tell more about a person by what she says about others than you can by what others say about her.

—AUDREY HEPBURN

Have you ever been surrounded by a group of gossiping girls, and the longer you sit there, the more outrageous the rumors become? If you said no, you would be unusual. At one point or another, most of us have been in this situation and most likely, we have all given our input. Sometimes that comes back to haunt us, because by telling the truth we might hurt someone unintentionally. Don't get me wrong. I used to occasionally add my two cents' worth, but it usually ended up doing more damage than good. That is why I developed my concept of keeping my mouth shut to the gossipers. Instead, I go straight to the person the rumor is about and clear the air. My dad puts it best: "You cannot argue with ignorance, and you cannot educate it." To be good in this world, you need to suck up your fears and speak up. Tell the group who is gossiping that rumors are hurtful, and then walk away. Yes, just keep walking, sister. Regardless of whether or not you know the rumor to be true, it's not your place to talk about it.

Being girls, the gossipers have probably experienced damaging rumors about themselves and know the repercussions. Don't be a part of the problem by hanging around to listen. Set an example. Then be a good friend to the person being gossiped about. Let the individual know that because you care about him or her and value the friendship, you want to share face to face what you heard or saw. Whatever you do, do not send a text. I have made this mistake— texting is the easiest way to have something misread! And, in all honesty, I've learned that it is the coward's approach.

As simple as that concept sounds, many of us never do this. Instead, it seems most of their brains are programmed to tell at least ten people before the rumor accidentally gets back to the person it's about, and they are then forced to confront the accusations. It is more beneficial in the long run to not be one of the rumormongers.

Once you find your circle, it's natural to talk about the popular gossip going on. But don't go opening your mouth to just any girl, because girls are not always nice. Many girls have chips on their shoulders that make them hate other girls like you. They use your words to hurt you. Unfortunately, a lot of us have been in this position. Girls have the stereotype of being enemies to each other. Can we please stop this stereotype? Can we instead build each other up and push each other to acquire our own successes? Some men expect us to be drama queens who let our emotions get involved in every decision we make or every word that comes out of our mouths. Quite frankly, with the issues I've had with girls, I don't think guys are that far off. But hopefully, like me, you love to prove guys wrong. Let's prove them wrong and build a society in which we tell girls and women that we like their outfits, praise each other for our accomplishments, and push each other on our off days. We can *be the change* by being the bigger person; keeping our mouths shut, and addressing the problem with another girl head-on.

In my field of work, I receive a lot of information about people. My favorite motto is, "Keep it off the record." Whatever information someone tells you cannot be printed or spread if they say, "Off the record." Let's start applying this to everything we do. When we hear gossip, let's assume it is off the record and not spread it. I have two best friends I can be off the record with at any time and fully trust that they will protect my deepest secrets.

I once was the girl who was too kind and believed everyone had a spirit like mine. I was crushed to find out that someone who I thought wanted the best for me was trying to ruin my reputation and spirit. She used my words against me and even twisted them. I was discouraged for about a day. Then I realized that I had spent too many hours on an irrelevant person who had not learned the meaning of *off the record*. This concept should apply in all your friendships. If your friend tells you something in confidence, it is not your place to tell other people. That is her business.

That's why I decided to simply keep my mouth shut. The good girl will come forward and confront her issues or speculations head-on. She won't stoop to be like other girls. She is not like them; she is powerful, kind, and determined. She doesn't have time to break other girls' spirits—nor does she want to. She is too busy breaking records. Be a record breaker, not a heartbreaker.

Social Girl's Things to Remember

- For one month, I vow my friends and I will avoid talking about others when we are together. *(It only takes one month to break a bad habit.)*
- I vow to rid myself of people who gossip more than they grow. *(It is a proven fact that you can pick up habits from those with whom you spend the most time.)*
- If I hear something about myself or someone else, I will talk face to face with the person before I react or spread rumors. *(Miscommunication is often the fuel for gossip.)*
- From now on, I refuse to attempt to defuse a situation through texting.

Dear Sunshine Girl,

She brought her own sunshine,
everywhere she went.

When I was a little girl, my mom used to sing, "You Are My Sunshine," anytime I was sad or sick. Like chicken noodle soup, that song always made me feel better. I think that is when I started to realize how powerful optimism is. By looking for the best in every situation, you set yourself up for success, and ultimately, days full of sunshine. Unfortunately, optimism is often scorned because it is not "cool" or someone finds it "annoying." I'll say this one time: there is nothing wrong with loving everything. There is something beautiful that comes from everything, even disasters. You're probably thinking, What about cancer? Natural disasters or terrorist attacks? All of those things are horrific in nature; however, cancer shows that we all have a fight in us, no matter how small. Natural disasters give us a chance to rebuild and refocus on what is important to us. Terrorist attacks teach us that no one can defeat our morale or unity. I've been affected by all of those tragedies, and at the end of the day, I'm still here. The horrible nightmares did not take away my hope. Every negative thing that has happened to you should make you optimistic, because you are still here and you overcame what many may have seen as an impossible situation.

As cheesy as it sounds, you can learn a thing or two from children. Children are blissfully ignorant of the hatred and hurt of the world. They fall down and then stand right back up. They have no fear, because they do not know the world can hurt them. Can you not use a little bit of that hope in today's world? I'm not asking you to be ignorant toward the issues of the world; I'm just asking that you do not let it steal your sunshine.

Equip yourself with positivity. You woke up this morning: one point for you. You have a roof over your head: another point for you. You have the opportunity to drive to a job or apply for one: another point for you. By the end of the day, you have mastered living rather than surviving. If you look at each small and insignificant opportunity you have daily, you cannot help but feel thankful for the life you have been given.

As you go out into the world each day, be a ray of sunshine. If you are naturally optimistic, you do not have to change when those around you are not. The world needs more sunshine, and they need a lot more girls like you who are willing to be rays of sunshine when everyone else is surviving under clouds.

P.S. It is a proven fact that you need Vitamin D to survive, and a major source of Vitamin D comes from the sun. The world needs you, sunshine girl.

Sunshine Girl's Things to Remember

- I vow to be the sunshine of my own life, because I am my best ally.
- I vow to never take rejection personally.
- I vow to never let a conversation turn to negativity.
- I vow to be myself and never compromise my happiness in order to fit in.

Dear Social Media Queen,

Branding is what people say about you when you are not in the room.

Social media has ruined not only women's confidence, but also our communication skills, love lives, and job opportunities. Don't get me wrong! I love social media, and my networks alone reach over two hundred thousand people, but I hate what social media has morphed us into. To me, there are four main categories that ruin the reputation of a good woman on social media: (1) Using your social media as a diary, (2) using it to bully other women, (3) using it to mess with relationships or pick up guys, or (4) using it to complain or add to an argument that you are clueless about, thus adding to the already blossoming speculation about women being dramatic, jealous bimbos.

Lets just start from the first problem, that of using social media as your diary. I know that after a long day, I love logging onto Facebook and seeing —— complain about how her water heater went out after she caught her boyfriend cheating on her with her cousin, after she came home from losing her job. If you cannot already tell, that was completely sarcastic! No one wants to log on and see that, and no one wants to be around that either. Truly strong women will not play victim. They will put on brave faces and work their butts off to change their circumstances. The same goes for social media. If you put your private problems on the Internet, they are accessible to everyone (regardless of whether your profile is private). Why would a guy want to date a girl who would air all his dirty laundry? That is why you should never be that girl. As a good girl, you don't want anyone feeling sorry for you, because pity means that people look at you as if you're pathetic, and you are *not* pathetic, honey.

Speaking of pathetic, bullies are the biggest cowards of the Internet. As stated earlier, this is the second-biggest problem with social media; it provides easy access to hate on other women without the woman being present. Nothing annoys me more than scrolling through my Instagram feed and seeing people comment on a picture about how fake or Photoshopped someone looks. News flash@jerk2day! No one cares what you think, you creep on her Instagram because you don't have the confidence to come out from behind your keyboard. As if guys are not harsh enough on social media, women can be just as bad. It all starts with *hints*. You know a girl is about to raise hell when she sub-tweets something referring to another girl. That is a form of bullying! Once you put something on the Internet, you can't take it back. It is there forever, and even if you find out that what you posted was not true, you still presented the entire world with a false rumor about a girl. By doing this, you might have ruined this girl's reputation.

I have the perfect example of bullying someone through social media, because it happened to me. When I was a freshman in high school, two girls made a YouTube video pretending to be me. In this video, a girl had a blonde wig on with a cowboy hat, and Taylor Swift was playing in the background. After that, the "wannabe me" drank a bottle of milk, and because I'm allergic, she started choking … you know what happens next. Obviously that did not faze me, because I'm still here. But, in essence, these things hurt. Once you put something on the Internet, it doesn't go away. Although that video was taken down, I could still access it if I really wanted to. As if bullies were not bad enough, lazy bullies who use the Internet are further adding to the issues women face daily in society. Do not use your social media for evil. Use it to promote yourself and others in the best possible light.

Let's shine a light on the next Internet problem, that of using social media to mess with relationships. Today we have so much emphasis on "relationship goals." We have access to writing people whom we know we shouldn't be writing. Texting made it easier to cheat, but social media has made it almost impossible to catch. It disappoints me when girls have the audacity to use social media to write guys who are in relationships. I have never been that girl, and I never will be. I'm going to keep this section short, because it is simple. Don't be a dirty girl. Stop using social media to pick up guys by posting pictures of yourself half naked and pretending to be someone you're not on the Internet. Ladies, you have to respect yourselves before you can demand that men respect you. Do not let guys have a lazy relationship with you. Better yet, don't let a *like* determine your self-worth. You are all beautiful women who were created for a special reason and for a special person. Don't go after someone who is already with his special person. Your guy is out there, but you're going to have to close your laptop and phone to find him. So put some clothes on, go make some money, and use your social media to build your brand.

The final issue with social media is that it allows the "experts" on every issue to voice their opinions, even if their opinions are completely false. Unfortunately, I feel like we have all been there at one point. Look at the world around you; it is full of negativity regarding every issue. As good, strong women, we don't need to push more negativity into the world; it's better to illuminate positivity through our posts. Especially if you are clueless about a subject, you know it is better to stay out of the argument. I'm involved in the sports industry, and anytime something happens within our sport, everyone jumps on the bandwagon to give his or her opinion. I often wonder whether women even take time to realize that their opinions do not matter to everyone. Unless you can directly influence something, you don't need to get in-volved—especially if it does not impact you at all. If it is not your business and you're not an expert, sit back and enjoy the posts; otherwise, someone out there will be reading your ridiculous post on an issue and laughing at your ignorance (Don't even give them a chance). Even I am guilty of getting involved, but I have learned my lesson. You don't have to be the smartest person in the room, but there is nothing wrong with being the smartest girl on the web.

The best philosophy in regards to the Internet is to never post anything that your grandma would gasp at or your boss would disapprove of. If that isn't enough of a warning, think about your child googling your name and finding pictures of you drunk, in a bikini, on spring break. *Yikes!* Be classy and be smart when you post. You never know whose hands it could end up in.

Social Media Queen's Things to Remember

- I vow to challenge my friends to put their cell phones in their purses or jackets when we are at dinner. I will engage in conversation outside of my phone screen.
- For every picture I post with a filter I will post another picture without a filter or photo touch-ups.
- Before I post, I will ask myself, "Is this a post that someone I truly love would be proud of?" If it is not, I will delete it; I respect myself too much to jeopardize a relationship or job because of a post online.
- I vow to start a journal, before I start sharing my personal business with the world.

- For one month, at every social event that I go to (concert, speaking engagement, sleepover), I will refrain from posting during the event so that I can focus on enjoying the moment.

Dear Young Girl,

Be soft; do not let the world make you hard. Do not let pain make you hate. Do not let the bitterness steal your sweetness.

$\mathcal{I}$f you are still in high school, I consider you young. I do not mean that as an insult. In fact, this is one of the most influential chapters of your life, but it is not the conclusion. When I was in high school, I believed that the drama was life altering and that the decisions I made in that very moment would not matter ten years later. I was so wrong.

In high school, we believe that the world revolves around us, and we neglect the outside world because we are so focused on ourselves. If I can offer you one important piece of advice, it would be to hold onto your innocence and respect your morals. It has to be so hard to grow up in a world that tells you that you should be wearing makeup in eighth grade and texting by the age of twelve. I understand that you are under a lot of pressure, but be smart. Your life is important, and a lot of people care about you.

Now is the time to make mistakes and be selfish, but do not make mistakes that will end up changing the rest of your life. I promise that your chances of hanging out with your high-school friends will change dramatically when you go to college. So study hard, and value your education. If you want to be a woman who is worth remembering, prove to the world that you are memorable. Stop being rude to your parents and family, because they are the people who are genetically connected to you, and they will love and support you even in your darkest moments. Remember that your parents are doing the best they can. It was not until I went off to college that I realized how much I really did need my parents. It is your parents' job to discipline you, and although it may be hard, they are doing it because they love you. If you do not have parents like that, have your own back. It will be harder, but I promise that the rewards for having self-respect will reflect in your future.

Lastly, stop trying to grow up so fast. You can look at these celebrities and see a mirage of what it is to be grown up, but it is not that glamorous. Cherish the time you have to be young! If you work tirelessly at this moment in your life, you'll thank yourself in ten years. This moment sets you up for the next step of your life. Don't talk about others, do not post ignorantly, and be careful. The world is extremely negative around you right now, and if you let it, it will make you into someone you don't deserve to be. Remember where you come from and the type of person that you want to be. Let her guide you and help you make the right decisions. You were meant for more. Do not let society tell you the way you should grow up.

Young Girl's Things to Remember

- I vow to respect my body.
- I vow to be a young woman who offers more to the world than just my existence.
- I vow to be a kid and not to stress about being perfect.
- I vow to get along with my parents.
- I vow to work hard in school.

Dear Smart Girl,

Intelligence will never stop being beautiful.

What makes a woman beautiful? It is not her curves or her looks; it is what she chooses to do with her life and image. There are two meanings of the word beautiful. To find a beautiful woman, you can walk on the street of any major city and they are a dime a dozen. But if you find one that truly radiates confidence and intelligence, she is a rare one indeed. That is the utmost form of beauty, in my opinion.

Is it not discouraging to you that it is a rarity to be both beautiful and smart? You may think that a man does not want a woman who is more intelligent than he is, but that is not true. A real man wants a woman who can teach him about her different beliefs, what she stands for, and how she perceives the world. If he wanted a bimbo to stand there and look pretty, he could go to

Toys"R"Us and pick up a Barbie. I'm telling you that it is possible to be a Barbie with a brain. Be a woman who contributes to society, questions the ways of the world, and sets out to explore herself in profound ways. Be a woman who has relevance and self-respect.

For decades society has expected women to be inferior to men. We were told we could not manage a team of men, play against men, or make a sound decision without letting our emotions get involved. I'm tired of that perspective of women, but nothing is going to change if we don't want it to. We need to stop trying to compete with men and start proving our worth through our actions. We use feminism as an excuse to blame society, when instead we should come together and work as a team that does not bash men or the ways of the world but tries to change those assumptions.

We are not ignorant, and ignorance is not bliss. Smart women who know what they want in this world are one of the most dangerous breed there is. You were made to be an intelligent woman, we all were. No matter where you are from or what your status is, your brain matters. Challenge yourself today to learn something that excites and frightens you. That is the best way to determine what you stand for. Be a woman who watches the news and is up to date with current events. Be a woman who does not dumb herself down to appease a man. Be a woman who brings new ideas to the table without making men feel sorry for her. Just be yourself, and think about what you say before you spit it out. Your mind is the most important asset of your being, and the amount of information it can absorb is incredible! If you want to be rare, be a woman who shows brains and beauty. The rest will follow.

Smart Girl's Things to Remember

- I vow to never question my intelligence.
- I vow to never let a guy dictate my mind.
- I vow to challenge the way the world thinks and think on my own.
- I vow to explore myself and learn more about myself every day.

Dear World Changer,

*There is no force more powerful
than a woman determined to rise.*

*O*ur world is constantly changing. With that evolvement comes a new role or expectation for what women are supposed to do or be. The world calls us feminists. However, as a woman, I see two types of feminists: femi*nasties* and girls that are femi*nice*. Personally, I am *feminice*. I am not knocking those who do the following, but I'm not marching, screaming, or showing violence to anyone in order to gain respect.

Let me explain. I'm not going to waste my time trying to get rights that I already have. By thinking we deserve more, we are really asking for special treatment. Is that not what we are trying to escape? We want to be treated the same, yet we are asking for things that are female generalized. Some examples are justice, gratification for being a female, or (my favorite) we need more female CEOs—but not more female soldiers, oil drillers, auto mechanics, or firefighters. Why is that? It is simple. Women do not find those jobs enchanting enough. Call me crazy, but why say you cannot get the same job as a man when you're not willing to do the dirty work required in the male-dominated fields? It's not that you cannot complete these jobs; it is just not your first choice. Did you know that during WWII women were needed to fill jobs that were traditionally occupied by men? In fact, during the war an estimated 350,000 women served in the US Armed Forces, both at home and abroad. They worked in factories, served as nurses, drove trucks, repaired airplanes, and worked as chemists and engineers, in order to keep America strong while the men were fighting. The irony? The Women's Airforce Service Pilots (WASPs), who flew planes from factories to military bases, won Congressional Medals of Honor in 2010. I'll admit that I smiled when I first heard that. Those women did not complete these jobs to receive recognition. They did it because they knew that they were needed, and they knew that it was for something much bigger than themselves. I see Rosie the Riveter signs and think about how tough it was to be a woman in that time period. One thing I learned from that is that class and talent will overcome gender any day of the week.

Before you go and tweet that I'm a sexist woman, think about what I said. Be a *feminice*. Your reputation will never suffer, because you are demanding equality that we are lucky enough to have. If you want to make more money as a woman, don't study interpretive poetry dance—study architecture, engineering, or computer programming. Your sex should never be an excuse; the only thing holding you back is yourself. If you truly think that you are oppressed, travel overseas to where women are not allowed to leave their homes, where their husbands are being chosen for them and rape is happening at a young age. There are countries where women are beaten for speaking and are not allowed the basic freedom of receiving an education. These women are not allowed any liberties—and some here are complaining that the President of the United States is going to take his time to oppress women? I hate to break it to you, but there is war, unemployment, poverty, and health-care issues; all those issues are affecting a lot more people than just you. In the most feminice way, if you think that living in America is hard as a woman, please stop and think of others. Think of the women during WWII or the women who are in the Middle East, Asia, Africa, and so many other unenlightened places. Think of the women who are overseas defending your freedom to go to school or get married to the man that you want and letting you have the freedom to speak. Those women are fighting for your freedom in countries where women are not even seen as human beings. That is bravery, and that is being a true feminice.

You are so blessed to be a woman in the United States of America. Why? Well, because you can get a quality education, wear a bikini at the beach, go out in public, or have a career and family. If that does not make you feel undefeatable, I do not know what will. It's time that as women, we stop asking for more and instead start working for more.

In case my personal opinion was not convincing enough, let's talk about common *feminasty* beliefs.

1. **Sexual objectification of women**. Several women demanding more respect often have been heard chanting or yelling inappropriate terms referring to parts of their bodies, because they believe that men do not respect a woman's body enough.
    *   AB Response: The same women are wearing lingerie in front of millions of fans, referring to each other as "b****," and asking their man to reward their good behavior with sex in their music. The way I see it, men will not respect women who do not respect themselves.

2. **Equality for all women.** Several feminasties believe that all women should be treated equally (I think some of us could agree with that notion), whether it be in the workplace or at home. They believe that, as women, we are all special humans.
    *   AB Response. The same women are cursing and shaming others into believing that they are sexist and ignorant for not thinking the same way they do. The ironic question is this: What makes me less of a woman if I don't think the way you do? As women, we should have the freedom to believe what we want and think for ourselves. That is equality.

I could keep going, but the point is that you do have equality. I refuse to believe that I am any less of a person because I am a woman. The female equality issue began because women wanted equal rights in legal issues, social settings, and basic governmental rights. Last time I checked, we had those rights. Woman to woman, you're a badass. Why? Because you can have children, you can wear heels or combat boots, you can wear makeup or be natural, you can have long or short hair. You have the choice to be whatever type of woman you want to be. Be a great one.

This topic is important to me. I do not want younger girls growing up thinking that being a woman is a flaw. Being a woman is a powerful thing. When the world is being hateful, be a feminice. Most importantly, lead by example and be a good role model to the next generation of powerful women. In the words of Rosie the Riveter, "We can do it."

World Changer's Things to Remember

- I vow to stand up for what I believe in, while still allowing others to make their own choices.
- I vow to think before I act, because I know how valuable or hurtful words can be.
- I vow to not objectify my body to prove a point.
- I vow to be a woman of purpose in every setting.
- I vow to set an example for generations to come.

Dear Busy Girl,

I refuse to be the girl who didn't pursue her passions because she did not know how to prioritize and organize.

ake it from the girl who took sixteen-plus hours a semester, was involved in five clubs, volunteered for everything, and took the term *overachiever* to the next level—you got this, busy girl! If you are spreading yourself a little thin, that means you're hustling. If you still have your youth and a big future ahead of you, you should be exhausted and hustling anyway. After all, you'll have time to sleep when you're dead. Let's discuss how you can manage your time, without becoming a zombie, okay?

First, find something that keeps you curious, that benefits your future, and that relieves stress. If you're attending anything else that you struggle to make time for weekly, drop it. Girls like us will not put our best efforts into something if we are not fully committed to it, whether it is guys or knitting class (assuming there are some knitters out there). If it does not make you happy or make you money, it is not worth doing. Stop overwhelming yourself because you are too afraid to say no. I learned this the hard way. When I graduated college and came down from the high, I was exhausted and did not want to do anything but sleep. Make sure you don't get so caught up in pleasing everyone and doing everything that you forget that *you* exist.

Second, color code. Before you roll your eyes, just hear me out. If someone is guiding you, it makes it easier to complete a task. For instance, I had a dry-erase calendar on the back of my door all through college. I used the blue marker for sorority events, the orange marker for school events, the pink marker for school work, and the yellow marker for work. I would go through each task every day by time slots, and I was able to stay on schedule without losing track of why I was doing it all in the first place. Find your own version of color coding and create a method for your madness. Force yourself to complete a task as soon as you receive it. Procrastination is the good girl's kiss of death; do not put off what can be done right away. I promise, *Grey's Anatomy* and Netflix will be there when you're done with the mandatory work.

Third, stop making life so hard on yourself. Do not stay up studying until four in the morning and drag into class exhausted and haggard, all because you waited until the last minute to study. You will not be able to focus on anything else except that one task, and it will make the rest of your day less productive. Also, do not dress like a hobo every day because you were too lazy to lay your clothes out the night before. Finally, do not make those around you miserable because you cannot handle the stress you brought on yourself. I hate to be the reality fairy, but you are in charge of your life, and you have to take responsibility for all of your actions. Ironically, you can have a chaotic life and still have it all together. Stop making excuses, and find a way to make each day easier. For example, you could start your coffee before you jump into the shower and drink it as you're getting ready. It will prevent any unexpected spilling of coffee while on the run and keep you from having coffee breath, because you'll brush your teeth before you leave the house. You'll feel energized before you arrive at work or school, which looks so much better than running in at the last minute with your hair flying everywhere, balancing coffee in one hand and your dignity in the other. There are so many ways to improve your quality of life when you multitask and do not put things off. Start with the easiest task, and find ways to make the days more progressive by making every task easy to comprehend and follow.

Finally, dance it out! Even the busy girl comes to her breaking point. To avoid letting that happen, let it out. Turn on some music and just dance. It is a proven fact that dancing can improve your mind-body connection. It helps promote chemical balance by reducing stress hormones, and it improves the production of endorphins. As Elle Woods stated, "Endorphins make you happy." Make time to metaphorically or physically dance alone, and you'll be able to tackle any task.

The key to having it all while doing it all is just knowing that you *can* do it. Do not overthink it; just stay positive and trust your capabilities. Right now, things may seem crazy or out of your control, but the best is yet to come, and although the world may throw a lot of things at you, the world cannot take away your passion. Get organized in your own way, and learn to say no. The world is yours, busy girl! Do not limit yourself, and take care of the most important person in your story—*you!*

Busy Girl's Things to Remember

- I vow to achieve one small goal a day for myself.
- I vow to say no when my schedule is too busy.
- I vow to stay prepared a day before.
- I vow to lay out my goals ahead of time and achieve them by working toward them every day.
- I vow to eliminate distractions.

Dear Beautiful Girl,

Admire someone else's beauty,
without questioning your own

Three billion women populate the world, and every single one of us is different (even twins have different fingerprints). We all have our own minds, and that is something that society tends to forget when they create their image of the perfect woman. Body shaming has taken over the world, and I have seen more hatred toward women for their makeup-free faces and the shapes of their bodies. Recently a story surfaced about a young women who is categorized as one of America's sexiest women; however, this story revealed that she had an ugly heart. This model was at the gym and snapchatted about an overweight woman naked in the shower, saying she was gross. Seriously? Another story revealed that a popular retail store is under fire for one of their saleswomen body-shaming a teenage girl as she was trying on clothes. If we are not safe at the gym or at the mall, where are we safe?

It is now the twenty-first century. Corsets have gone out of style, and anorexia and bulimia have started trending. How disappointing is that? Torturing yourself is never worth the benefit of being thin or improving the appearance that someone else has said is flawed. You are not flawed; you are rare and beautiful. As if women do not have enough pressure on them, we add in the pressure to look a certain way. It takes all types of women, with all types of body shapes, to make up this world. As a good girl, you do not look down on anyone; you want to see your sisters happy and healthy. Figure out what your happiness goal is, and work hard to attain it. Success does not take days off. Everyone faces battles when it comes to self-esteem. I'm here to help you conquer those inner demons and turn them into your biggest fans. It's story time!

There once was a little girl who did not see herself the way that others did. She saw herself as a warrior princess who was going to be a famous movie star. While others looked at this girl with doubt because she was overweight, she kept dreaming and writing Oscar-worthy speeches. She was the happiest elementary school student there was, until her teacher started pointing out her flaws. This teacher was an attractive blonde who favored those who looked like she did. She could not open her heart to the beauty of being different from one another. The teacher did not know that the little girl was sick and going to the doctor weekly complaining of stomach pain and inflammation. It was not until the end of third grade that the girl found out she was severely allergic to milk. She had been slowly poisoning herself by eating dairy products daily. Once the little girl cut dairy out of her diet, she instantly lost weight and was without pain for the first time in her life. Fast-forward to high school, and the once-overweight little girl decided to go to a concert in her old town. One of her former classmates recognized her and was in utter shock at how she had turned out, not just in her appearance but also in her heart.

That girl was me, Alexis Bloomer. I started off as a young girl who battled sickness and inflammation, and now I'm writing a book encouraging you to love yourself at every stage. I want you to know that if you're dealing with depression because of your appearance, you are not alone. I still struggle with my self-esteem at times; it is human nature. However, I want to dig deep and find out what is stealing our happiness in regard to our appearance.

Are you overweight? If you are, is it because you cannot help your situation or because you are hopeless? I recently tried to start working out daily (previously it had been weekly), and I realized how intimidating it was at the gym. There are crazy machines and people of all ages and levels; it is a tad overwhelming. But no matter how out of place you feel, do not give up. Do not be afraid to start at the bottom and ask for help. The people who truly promote positive body image want to see you succeed. The working out has helped me become the warrior princess I always knew I was.

I challenge you to start small and work hard on your happiness when it comes to improving your health. Do it for yourself. Do not do it for society, because society is greedy and will never be pleased. There are women in Hollywood who are loved for being exactly who they are. Melissa McCarthy was told she would never make it as a star because she was overweight. But, like all of us, she loves to prove people wrong. Now she has her own clothing line and is one of the most popular actresses in Hollywood. I could go on and on about ladies who have been successful in their own ways. But what it comes down to is that you have to love yourself before anyone else can love you.

Confidence is sexy in every size.

Are you insecure about your height? I'm short, while all of my friends are tall. Picture Baby Gap meets runway model, and you have figured out how different we look walking together in public. I wear heels every day, and it makes me feel more comfortable with who I am, but not all short girls feel comfortable doing this. I say, embrace what you have. If you are short, the rain hits you last, and you'll always win at hide-n-seek. If you're tall, you can reach things on the top shelf and can walk less steps. Consider this: Olympic gold-medal gymnast Simone Biles is 4'9", and Olympic gold-medal swimmer Katie Ledecky is 5'11". Guess what? They are both badass and both competing at the Olympics. Each woman is different in height and body shape but has earned the same gold medal for different events. Your height does not determine your heart. We are all created for a reason, and intelligent people know not to define us by how many inches we stand—because girls like us are always going to have our heads in the clouds as we reach for stars.

Confidence is sexy at every height.

Right now in our country people are trying to divide us based on the color of our skin. However, we know that every skin shade is beautiful, and we will not give in to the hatred or division. I have friends of all races. All of us have struggled or felt left out because of our ethnicity at one point or another. Imagine the world in an array of colors, and now look at all the people through a sepia filter. All of the sudden we do not look that different, do we? My parents raised me to look past the color of the skin and embrace the depths of people's hearts. As good girls, we already see the world with its diverse beauty. I do not care about the color of your skin- you are beautiful. We are all women, and that universally unites us and gives us something to celebrate. Our cultures divide us, but our sex unites us.

Confidence is sexy in every color.

The main message is to just love yourself. Stop comparing yourself to the girls you see on Instagram. They have filters too. Do not talk yourself into plastic surgery, if you are doing it to fit in. If you like makeup, rock it. If you like the feeling you have after the gym, reward yourself daily by going back. Just look in the mirror and be pleased that God thought the world needed someone like you. The good girl would never allow herself to feel hatred toward her body. She would work hard to improve the character of the person she sees in the mirror.

The biggest ally—and hypocrite—you have is yourself. The world cannot define beauty by objects on one's body. Even the most beautiful women in the world have insecurities due to society's expectations.

For all of those good girls who asked me to address learning to love yourself by getting healthy (physically and mentally) check out that gorgeous person in the mirror. Thank your lucky stars that you have the honor to be her every day.

Beautiful Girl's Things to Remember

- I vow to find one attribute I love about myself every day.
- I promise to compliment another woman daily, without questioning my own beauty.
- I vow to take care of myself and my body.
- I will ignore the tabloids that tell me that I am not perfect. I will instead realize that my body and my beauty is one of a kind and irreplaceable.

Dear Trendsetter,

*No one is you, and that
is your power.*

This chapter is for all you women who are absolutely killing it in your careers, relationships, and life in general. Luckily I've been blessed to be this woman. I've worked hard to make sure that everything was successful that I invested my time into. With that have come the copycats. In my situation, it was girls who saw me hosting my own talk show and receiving free clothes, shoes—anything you can imagine. I wish more than anything that these girls could have been there when I was holding cords in the studio while another girl anchored or seen all the times that I had to sacrifice something to become successful or, even better, go stand in a storm to report on a football game. It is not all glamorous, and I think that statement is true for any profession. Anybody can do what I'm doing, but I don't think many are willing to put in the work to obtain it. That is the problem with our generation: they all want everything now, without putting in the hours. Discouraging as that mentality is, I still help girls when they ask for advice, because I wish someone had helped me when I was first starting out.

The world is full of followers, because it is easier to copy someone else than it is to make your own legacy. If you haven't noticed, technology has given several girls false ideas of how they are supposed to look and act. If you don't believe me, let me tell you a story about how easily girls are willing to change who they are based on some Internet personality. One of my friends stalks a certain makeup artist on both YouTube and Instagram and talks about how perfect she is and how she wants to look like her. At one point, she started to do her makeup in her style, dress like her, and even copy her poses in pictures. If you have been this person, I want you to know that by being yourself, you are enough.

If that story wasn't enough, let's talk about imitation on a global level. When Kylie Jenner posted a video about how to plump your lips using a cup, girls jumped on the bandwagon, resulting in injuries and swelling for many of them. Why is society encouraging girls to neglect who they are and their health, just to fit in? I'm not judging these girls, but I'm disappointed that fitting in is what society considers worthy of approval. I say, don't give society the satisfaction of owning you!

I know for a fact that all of you girls reading this book are probably like me in the fact that you hate to see another girl in public wearing the same bikini as yours or, heaven forbid, showing up in the same dress as you to a formal. Imitation is the same thing. Think of it this way: when you intentionally copy someone because you think it will transform you into her, you become the girl that intentionally wore the same dress as another girl to the prom. In my opinion, that is so tacky, but several of us do it because we feel like we have to in order to fit in. By being one of a kind- you already fit in with the Good Girl Movement.

Life works the same way. Seeing someone successfully doing or wearing something and then going out and trying to copy it discounts the person you truly are. Instead, you should blaze the trail your own way and stir up the pot by adding more competition to the already-competitive world of being a woman. The good girl would want to be a trendsetter in a classy way, not try to be someone else. In a world full of so many stereotypical girls, it is always refreshing to see a girl being herself. You are irreplaceable and one of a kind—don't ever let anyone tell you differently.

Trendsetter's Things to Remember

- I vow to remain authentic.
- I vow to be myself.
- I vow to make my own statement.
- I know that I am one of a kind and irreplaceable.

Dear Miss Almost Famous,

*The powerful women don't explain
why they want respect. They
simply don't engage with those
who do not give it to them.*

In our generation, we look up to celebrities who receive national attention and fame from making a sex tape. Why would we ever endorse or idolize a woman who exploits her body and uses it to gain national attention? I'm hoping that after you read that last sentence you were slightly embarrassed that we do idolize women who have not offered anything valuable to the world. I'm not looking down on anyone, I understand that sometimes you have to make sacrifices to achieve success. If it comes down to that, make decisions on your own terms.

If we cannot find a woman who we believe climbed the ladder to success fully clothed, then we must become one such woman. I know what you are thinking: "That is boring. Her life is more exciting, and I'm just a college girl or middle-aged woman who lives in a small town." This is where you are absolutely wrong. If you do not think that every particle of your genetic makeup is one of a kind and worthy of being worshipped, I'm here to give you a news flash. I'm not going to give you a lesson on the birds and the bees, but I do want you to know that every time you exploit who you are, you're becoming more attractive to the wrong men and less attractive to the right one. Which one do you really want?

If you do not care about the guys and you just want the national attention from anyone who will glance your way, you're putting yourself in the position to be the sex-tape girl. Any self-respecting woman would not want her legacy to be her performance in bed. Nor would she want to be remembered for her revealing pictures instead of her natural talent.

Don't be like the rest of them—be the exception. To do this, you have to stop trying to be something you are not. Stop trying to grow up so fast. Be a woman who is worth looking up to in this day and age. Lastly, learn from your mistakes—we all make them—no one expects you to be perfect, just do your best to be the best person you know. The way to do that is not to sell your reputation and morals to appease the society surrounding you.

Almost-Famous Girl's Things to Remember

- I vow to build my own dreams, not try to accomplish someone else's.
- I know that I am important when I am just being myself.
- I vow to stop trying to fit in and instead find a group that I fit into by just being myself.
- I vow to stop comparing myself to others.

Dear Confused Girl,

*When I feel a little low, I
put on my favorite high heels
to stand a little taller.*

—DOLLY PARTON

As women we have all stumbled for a moment and forgotten how amazing we truly are. We've let jealousy occupy our minds if only for a second. Jealousy is inevitable, and it is often confusing for a girl who has her life together and is accomplishing all of her goals. Why would we be jealous when we have everything? The answer is simple: strong women always want more. However, we have to learn how to achieve more without wanting what someone else has.

The way I look at it is this: God made me in a unique way, and at times he tests me, but he always wants what is best for me. He didn't create me to be like anyone else. He gave me the blessings I have because he knew that I would do the right thing with them. I'll put it in perspective. Every time you get jealous of someone else, think of the following: There are three other girls who would do anything to have your looks, your job, your intelligence, your family, your friends, your clothes, your car, and more. You have a quality or personal touch to you that other people want as well. Don't take it for granted, because there is another girl out there working 24/7 to attain what you have.

It is hard not to be jealous sometimes, and it doesn't make you a bad girl. It just makes you human. Instead of being jealous of each other, we should encourage each other, congratulate each other, and brag about each other.

As I mentioned, I've always been a woman who would help out someone who wanted to do an interview or ask me questions or for advice. Yes, I realize that those girls are the next generation of women and they want to take my job, but that just makes me want to work ten times harder to prove that I am here for a reason.

You were put in your position in life for a reason. You were not born in someone else's body, because no one else could handle the gifts that you have been given. Instead of getting jealous, use that emotion to motivate you to improve yourself. If you want what someone else has, you will miss out on the opportunities you have been given at that moment.

The good girl does not worry about being someone else, because she is too busy loving who she is. To be that type of woman, you have to always focus on bettering yourself. You should not be going through life competing with anyone, because the biggest competition you have is the woman who looks back at you in the mirror. Stop worrying about others and worry about improving yourself. It all starts with a positive mindset and self-love. Today I want you to remember that you are not a jealous woman! You are too busy loving yourself and encouraging other women to concern yourself with being jealous.

Confused Girl's Things to Remember

- I vow to stop myself before jealousy makes me negative.
- I vow to give people chances before I compare our accomplishments.
- I vow to stop judging myself, because I'm not the same as someone else.
- I vow to trust others until given a reason not to.
- I vow to cheer on other women!

Dear Selfless Girl,

*She cared about others, but she knew
she was worth caring about too.*

Two incredible women that I have the honor of knowing are the most giving and kind people I have ever met. They would give the shirts off their backs to someone who stabbed them in the back. They do not keep score or hold grudges. They move on and continue to share their love of the world with people who sometimes do not deserve it. They taught me that there is a difference between being selfless and being used. Unfortunately, the world often confuses the two words and burns both ends of the candle for those who care too much. Do not become that girl, the girl who uses someone else or lets others use her.

When people are selfless, they often neglect their feelings to benefit someone who would not do the same for them. It is bad when friends are taking advantage of you, but it is even worse when it is happening at home as well. Do not let it continue. Do not let anyone borrow money that you earned because they've spent theirs. Do not let them infringe on your schedule when they are not conscious of how valuable your time is. Do not let them hold you back.

Cinderella cleaned and cooked for three ungrateful women, while she lived in rags and only socialized with mice. When she realized her worth, she ended up finding the man of her dreams—and also got a killer pair of shoes. We are taught this lesson from a young age, yet we still fail to see the underlying messages of these children's stories: when we break away from what everyone else wants us to do, we end up finding ourselves and our strengths. Pocahontas let her natural curiosity get the best of her and brought together opposing forces. Mulan broke the stereotype and used her selflessness to defeat a villain. These are the stories we should be applying in everyday life. It is not about getting the prince at the end of a story; it is about focusing on what we want, even if others are trying to tell us what *they* want. Our stories matter too! I used the analogy of Disney princesses because they teach us to search for our princes in life—but the creators of those movies hid many messages under the surface that teach us to break free from other people's wants and discover our own.

There are so many women who were used for other people's glory, and I refuse to let you become one of them. That is why I put this chapter before the chapter about falling in love.

I used to put others' wants before my own, and in a lot of ways I still do. But I've realized that my dreams are worthy of time and people who do not use my selflessness for their own gratification. There is nothing wrong with being the girl who puts everyone else first, but realize that every now and then you deserve to be put first too.

If you forget about yourself, you're going to lose your unique spark—and yourself, if you are not careful.

In college I knew a pretty girl who changed friends and boyfriends like underwear, daily. I used to wonder why she had a new best friend weekly and why she could not seem to manage relationships. It became clear after I hung out with her for a few days. She talked about herself and her own problems constantly and failed to ever ask me how I was feeling. I soon stopped caring about her feelings, because they were all I heard about. Like a broken record, she kept bringing up the same things. Even though she was pretty, she struggled to see past herself. Being around her was exhausting and made me start to want to talk about myself all the time to other friends—because she never gave me a chance to say anything about myself. The same is true in relationships. If they are exhausting, you'll start to reflect their attitude to those closest to you. It is true what they say: *you are who you surround yourself with.* That is why it is so important to surround yourself with selflessly selfish people. Let me explain. You want someone who is willing to help you when you're in need but who also values his or her alone time and prior plans. Believe it or not, you can be giving and still do what is best for yourself.

Find people who balance you out and allow you to also be selflessly selfish. Learn that your happiness is just as important as making everyone else happy. Every day, I want you to do something for yourself, whether it is working out, reading, writing, or cooking … whatever. Anything that is totally yours is good. I'm asking you to be selflessly selfish, to be the girl who is there for others but also expects the same in return. So, selfless girl, remember that *you* matter too!

Selfless Girl's Promises

- I will learn to say no.
- I know that I cannot change the world, but I can change myself and be there more for myself.
- I will finally put myself first in my life.
- I know that I have to learn to serve myself before I can genuinely serve others.
- I will do things that make me happy every day.

Dear Girl in Love,

*It takes an extremely powerful man
to be with a powerful woman.*

When a girl falls in love, the world around her suddenly appears more beautiful. I don't quite understand it, but I do know that as women we look forward to life a lot more when we are getting to share our feats with someone. Indeed (fun fact), my hairdresser even told me that love can attribute to hair growth.

I hope that if you do fall in love, you fall for a man who values your drive and your talent, a man who encourages your curiosity and pushes you to become the woman you've always dreamed of being. However, many of us are going to go through a love that drains us. That type of love is so one sided that we forget we even had a dream. I'll just go ahead and say it: If your man does not support you in whatever path you choose, then he does not truly love you. I know that it is a harsh reality, but I learned through my own mistakes that if a man tries to keep you from becoming yourself completely, then he does not really love you for you; he loves you for the moment.

A man who appreciates your talent and craft will be your most loyal supporter. He will be by your side as you chase your dreams and do everything in his power to make it work, regardless of the hours and pay. As good girls, a lot of us tend to fall easily—or at least I did. Until I found the guy I am with now, I believed that love should be work. Let me tell you, any relationship worth having should be easy and challenging for *both* parties. You shouldn't have to worry about what he thinks about your new promotion, and you shouldn't be afraid to tell him when you get a bonus. The good girl deserves a guy who celebrates his woman's accomplishments and does not make her feel bad about who she is. If you are with someone right now and you do not know whether he is the one, ask yourself these questions:

1. Does he wish you good luck every time you have an important test, presentation, or interview?
2. Does he calm you down when you are under pressure and offer to help?
3. Does he get nervous for you? (Trust me, anyone who gets nervous for your big moments truly cares.)
4. Does he let you vent and get sassy when the weight of the world is on your shoulders?
5. Does he realize that your future and end goal is important to you?

6. Does he promise to give a solid effort no matter where you might move?
7. Does he make you feel safe and comfortable?
8. Does he know your comfort food when you have a bad day?
9. Does he encourage you to take care of your body and your mind?
10. Do your parents like him?

Trust me, the last one is the most important! Regardless of your relationship, your parents can often see through the lovesick puppy and see the man for what he truly is. At twenty-three years old, I realized that my parents were right.

Essentially, being the woman you are, you're going to take time, because you're probably very stubborn. You need to find a man who is driven in his own field but is patient enough to love you for the woman you are. If he ever makes you question yourself, he is not the one. When the good girl falls in love, she is fiercely loyal and vulnerable. However, with the right man, she doesn't have to worry about being hurt; she will always feel safe with him. Now ask yourself, are you with someone who makes you better? If you are, the only thing you'll have to worry about is being yourself and chasing your dreams, because the right guy knows that you were meant for great things.

#GoodGirl Rules of Love

- I vow to remain true to myself and be with someone who likes me the way I am.
- I vow to not put my career on hold to chase a guy, unless it's what I really want.
- I vow to not lose myself when I am in a relationship.
- I vow to not be so critical in relationships and to accept his flaws if they are not self-deprecating.

Good Girl Etiquette Tips

Class never goes out of style.

Etiquette is a lost art in today's society; however, it still is imperative. These basic tips may seem silly, but being a lady is a powerful tool. If you were never a debutante, you probably were not taught these ideals. Take these simple but effective tips, and apply them every day. The #GoodGirl has poise and grace.

Simple Rules for Dinner Engagements

- If you're a guest at someone's house (even your parents), offer to help with dinner. This simple gesture is considered polite, even if the host declines.
- Always clean up your mess; don't leave your plate for the host to clean up.

- The cell phone has no place at the dinner table. Be present in the conversation.
- Never show up to a party empty-handed, unless you were instructed to do so. A simple bottle of wine, dessert, or side dish is acceptable and sometimes welcomed.
- Chew with your mouth closed, even when chewing gum.
- This one is for my mom: Be sure to keep your elbows off the table while eating.
- It's probably best not to play with your food if you do not like it.
- Always say thank you to the cook or host. Being gracious is always in style.

Basic Everyday Etiquette

- Manners are incredibly important, especially in today's society. These words still matter:
  - Please
  - Thank you
  - Excuse me
  - Sorry
- Watch your mouth. At times it's hard not to curse. However, profanity as a second language is frowned upon. You are intelligent enough to express words without dropping the F-bomb.
- Hygiene is still important. I'm a fan of dry shampoo, but don't go three weeks without showering simply out of laziness. Find a nice perfume that you like. (It doesn't have

to be expensive, but the extra effort is worth it.) There are a few basics of hygiene:

- – Brush your hair before you leave the house.
- – No biting your nails.
- – Shaving is still a thing, in case you're wondering.
- – Brush those pearly whites.

- Cover your mouth when you sneeze, preferably into the crook of your elbow.
- Be considerate of others around you. For instance, talking on your phone in an elevator or yelling across the store to find your friend are no-nos.
- Always walk with confidence.
- A #GoodGirl can handle a crisis without drama, rise to the occasion in any situation, and be a leader. For instance, if you're a bridesmaid, it's your job to help the bride.
- Make an effort to be on time and dependable.

Social Settings

- Watch your alcohol intake. Trust me, you don't want to be the person who is made fun of or, worse, can't remember the next day what happened.
- Sometimes when you take in liquid courage your voice becomes more courageous as well. You don't have to be loud to be noticed.
- Whatever you do, please, please, please do not take your heels off at the bar or when leaving the bar. Wear the pain,

and then, next time, reconsider wearing heels if you're not comfortable in them.

- At the bar, I always hear guys making fun of the girls slow-dancing together. It's not weird to ask someone to dance. Give it a try.

Dress to Impress

- During job interviews, first impressions matter. I have had several girls apply to work at my business. When going to a job interview, it's best to look appropriate, cover your hair extensions, and put effort into your appearance.
  - **Do** be formal and professional; dress for the job you want to land. Try a suit (jacket with pants or skirt) or a simple dress in black or navy. Simple black pumps and pearls never go out of style. This is different for every occupation, but if you feel classy, you'll look classy.
  - **Don't** wear jeans of any sort, flip-flops, shorts, fishnet stockings, wild makeup, low-cut shirts, overly tight-fitting clothes, or noisy jewelry. My friend and fellow business owner said that crazy nails are also a dead giveaway that you are not comfortable in a position of power.
- My mom's magic rule is to always iron your clothes. Wrinkles represent laziness. I interviewed a celebrity once who said that the biggest turn-off is a girl showing

up for a date with wrinkles in her shirt. Trust me, people notice.

Dating Etiquette

- When meeting the parents, be sure to put your phone away. Even if you're listening, it still appears that you don't really care.
- College girls will hate me for this, but leave the oversized T-shirts and Nike shorts at home when visiting the parents for the first time.
- As a rule of thumb, it's probably best to not bring up old relationships.
- Also, it's not advisable to send ten text messages after the date and definitely not good to text during the date.
- Please do not break up by text; everyone deserves the decency of at least a phone call. Text messaging is the coldest form of communication.
- Try not to express feelings via text or Facebook post.
- Always be respectful on first dates, because it takes courage from both parties to show up for a date.

Thank-You Note Etiquette

A simple thank-you note can deliver a powerful statement. A handwritten letter is personal and shows appreciation far more than a text message or e-mail. When should you send a thank-you note? Definitely for wedding gifts, graduation gifts, baby showers, bridal showers, birthday gifts, when someone hosted a party in your honor, for donations, when someone has taken the time to introduce you to a possible employer, or for those who helped with a funeral.

I write thank-you notes anytime someone takes the time to send me flowers, write me a recommendation letter, or provide me with an internship, award, or scholarship. I also write thank-you notes when a boutique sends me clothes to wear. Simple acts of kindness go a long way.

How to Write a Thank-You Note

1. Start with a greeting:

Dear Good Girl,

2. Express thanks:

Thank you so much for the ——
I smiled when I opened ——.

3. Add specifics:

It meant so much to me that you threw a party in my honor.
The flowers brightened up my new office.
I love my new purse, and I cannot wait to show it off.

4. Extend follow-up:

I look forward to seeing you in the near future.
I hope to see you again soon.
I hope to come up and visit you soon.

5. Restate your thanks:

Thank you so much again for the thoughtful gift.
Thank you for your kind words.

6. End appropriately:

Sincerely,
Thank you,
With regards,
With love,

Effort is attractive! These simple tips will help you become the #GoodGirl you were meant to be. It might sound like a lot, but once you apply it to your everyday life, it will become simple.

Dear #GoodGirl

*B*efore you set off to conquer the world, surround yourself with exceptional women who motivate you to be the best woman in business and in life. The #GoodGirlMovement is made up of women who have battled several of the same issues that you have. By telling their personal stories, they are hoping to inspire other women to learn from their experiences.

Dear Good Girl,

I was definitely classified as a "good girl" too in high school. My mom is a teacher and my dad is a professor, so there was no partying or drinking. However, I still was a social butterfly. Growing up, I was extremely involved in sports and extracurricular activities. I was class president and was crowned prom queen. I'm not telling you this to brag but instead to break a stereotype. A tanned bleach blonde can become a successful and respected professional.

After high school I attended Texas A&M and graduated with my bachelor's. I had no idea what I wanted to do when I graduated, so I attended Sam Houston State University to receive my master's. After completion of my master's, I decided to take the highest-paying job I could find and just go for it. I moved and began working for Target as an assistant store manager. The store I worked at was the largest-volume Target store in the state of Texas, and I was in charge of money, customer services, and all the cashiers. I went from being a master's student to managing up to a hundred employees in the holiday season, within two weeks. To this day, I have no idea why I was given such a large responsibility at such a young age. I was working holidays and weekends and missing friends' and family's events. Honestly, the lifestyle was not of interest to me whatsoever, and I was not passionate at all about my job.

One day my dad, being a professor, sent me a job opportunity at a construction company. I applied for an accounting position, which I was qualified for after my year-long career in retail, handling $8,000,000+. I started as an accountant and worked hard to climb the ladder, and in 2015 I was given the opportunity to become a project manager for the first time. I hustled on this project and was given more and more opportunities to complete other jobs. I finally found a career that I loved! The best part? I found out that I was the first female project manager the company had ever hired. To realize that I broke down all those barriers is liberating.

In the construction field there are few women involved in any spectrum. I have been met with skepticism. I do not think that some men in construction necessarily respect a woman under thirty telling them what to do. In one situation, I called a subcontractor several times, and there was no response. I had to go sit in with my boss, and together we called and addressed the situation. My boss had my back and told the subcontractor that everything was to go by me. I appreciated that more than my boss will ever know.

In my industry, my perseverance is working. Our company just hired another female project manager, and with my hard work I feel like I am breaking down barriers and helping the next girl in line.

Others may be smarter, prettier, taller, skinnier, or funnier than me, but they can't outwork me.

If I could give you any advice, it's to find your talent in life and realize it's not always singing, dancing, or cooking. You can do anything you set your mind to.

Sincerely,
Samantha, 27, Texas
First Female Project Manager

Dear Good Girl,

I have really dug deep and decided that I would stand tall and tell you my story. Bullying is real, and it does not discriminate. If you or someone you know is being bullied, talk to someone. I promise, there are people that care.

I was bullied really bad in high school and thought that something was wrong with me. I had a hard time making friends, and I became depressed. I was the new girl in a small town on an Indian reservation. I did not grow up with these girls and most of them had known each other their whole lives. I was "different."

My sophomore year, I did something completely out of character: I lied to my parents. I had been invited to a party, and I thought, *This is it. They like me, or they wouldn't have invited me.* I was wrong.

I was jumped by four girls, which resulted in a fractured jaw, broken nose, and a shattered eardrum. I was devastated, embarrassed, hurt, and so much more.

After that experience, I made a promise to myself—a promise that I have worked so hard since that day to fulfill. I promised that (a) I would *never* allow another female to treat me that way, and (b) I would never make another woman feel the way that those girls made me feel.

I was raised in a very Christian home. I believed in God, but I still went with the flow of what everyone else around me was doing. I began lying to those I loved (my parents) about places I was going and who I was with. I did things I would never do, to impress people who in the big scheme were not good for me. After my accident, I dug deep into my faith. The closer I got to God, the more I loved myself. I see beautiful women everywhere I go. I challenge myself to compliment those women, to make them feel good enough to hopefully share the love with someone else. I never understood why we, as women, know the pain we can endure from other women, but we continue to still be so unkind. It makes no sense.

I am overjoyed with the #GoodGirlMovement, because now we are never alone.

Sincerely,
Mkenzee, 23, Louisiana
Social Networking Manager

Dear Good Girl,

Growing up, I always knew I was different in the sense that I knew I was set aside to do something different and make an impact on others. However, at a young age, I did not know how I would do that.

One of my defining moments was when I was a freshman in high school and a senior volleyball player came and helped us freshman out during practice. Then she came to our games and cheered us on as if we were on the varsity team. Right then I knew I wanted to be like that. So I set out to encourage and support others in their dreams, no matter what stage they were at.

I think it is so important to lift others up rather than tear them down. I also think that it is beyond important to show others that by being themselves they can be lights. That is why I started my blog.

Yes, I am the preacher's daughter and a goody two shoes, but I am proud of that now.

In high school, I really struggled. My junior and senior year I was clinically depressed and was on medication for depression and anxiety. I would struggle some days so badly that I wouldn't want to go on. However, I would never act upon those thoughts, because in the hard times I would always hear a voice in my head telling me I was created for more than this.

Once I graduated, I still struggled off and on, but I ended up meeting my two best friends, who believed in me and loved me for me. I slowly began to build my confidence and became the peppy and bubbly woman I am today. We all have struggles in life, but it is how we react to them and how we stand against them that defines us. We have to choose to be the victors and not the victims of our own lives.

Xoxo,
Hannah, 31, Colorado/Texas
Photographer and Blogger

Dear Good Girl,

I was born and raised in Southern California and educated in Arizona. I am the owner and operator in a male-dominated field, parking lots in downtown San Diego.

I have to be confident, resilient, and hardworking. This is not just a job, it's a lifestyle. Parking lots are open twenty-four hours a day and seven days a week. I am the accountant, tech support, property maintenance, and serve as security. But I love what I do, and I fight hard for my company, because if I didn't I wouldn't be successful.

The skills that I get to use on a daily basis come from many walks of life.

Confidence. I am a first-generation cowgirl, and I was Miss Rodeo California. This was one of the best years of my life, because it gave me the necessary confidence to be in the public and handle any situation that has been thrown my way.

Resilience. I believe I learned this by growing up in the rodeo arena. Being a first-generation cowgirl, I had to get up anytime

I was knocked down. I had to learn how to rope and ride all at the same time. It's still something that I have to work at today. I still face challenges, but my resilience kept me going and got me to where I am today. In 2015 I won over $160,000 at team roping's (male-dominated events), a feat that only a few have accomplished, in just one trip to the event.

Hard work. I have a major in political science and a minor in Spanish from Arizona State University. I had to work hard in college. It did not come easy for me. Also, when you add on maintaining good grades and competing on weekends, it took dedication.

I am a successful woman in a male-dominated field. I believe a good pair of heels or work boots will make you stand a little taller. And above all, I believe that kindness and how you treat others still matters. Keep charging and never give up.

Sincerely,
Markie, California
Business Owner

Dear Good Girl,

A while ago, a dear and wonderful friend of mine posted a picture of me with my two-year-old son. All I could notice was how round my face looked. I spent all morning losing my mind, wondering how I could allow myself to get that way. My poor boyfriend spent a large amount of the day convincing me that I was perfect the way I was.

The tears fell anyways, and I didn't touch anything except water until around two that afternoon. Then this picture came up with an old post in my memories on Facebook. I was ninety-eight pounds and extremely unhealthy for my five-foot-six-inch frame; I had a BMI of 16—and 18.9 is considered underweight. In this picture my neck was sunken in, the skin on my arms was just hanging where I'd once had muscle, I had no meat; I was just skin and bones. My coloring was dull, and my hair had started falling out.

Anorexia was never something I planned. I had just left an abusive marriage in which rail thin was always ideal. The skinnier the better, to make up for the stretch marks I'd "allowed" myself to get during pregnancy. With the stress of my divorce, I had no desire to eat, ever. I ate enough to continue breastfeeding—all calories went into my body to fight to make milk for my son.

Now, over a year later, at a healthy 125 pounds (still very thin), I continue to struggle with what I see sometimes. My view of what is normal has become skewed. The roundness of my hips, the fact that you cannot count my ribs, my resistance to buying a size 3/4 instead of a 00/0, my now-closed thigh gap, and even my rounder face are all signs of health but also reminders that I am no longer what I was. I'm healthier, happier, and more energetic, but I have to keep recovering. I will fight the urge to crash, and I will enjoy eating. The image of perfection that was pushed on me by a very sick and angry man is losing its hold on me. I'm able to finally love myself, stretch marks, soft hips, and all.

Sincerely,
Katie, 23, Texas
Substitute Teacher

Dear Good Girl,

I grew up being bullied, because I was the overweight girl with asthma, and I could not run. I was extremely self-conscious about how I felt in my own skin. I genuinely felt unattractive and felt that no guy would ever like me. I started to believe what everyone was saying about me.

My sophomore year, I was out most of the year with gallbladder issues. Yet the bullying was still there. I came back to school my junior year to rumors that I had died. I ended up leaving public school and started a charter school, where I discovered my love of writing. All the bullying I endured hurt me, but that all changed when I met someone who made me change the way I looked at myself.

Now, I'm nineteen, five foot four, curvy, and proud. I have my own blog, got my license. I still struggle in the dating department, but I am happily living my life being comfortable in my own skin.

The best advice I can give you, beautiful girl, is to always be confident in yourself. You were not put on this earth to please others. You were put on this earth to grow and do what is best for *you*! So you weren't born to be skinny as a twig; that is okay. So you were not born to be tall; there is absolutely nothing wrong with your height. Always be proud of who you are and how you look. Your opinion and how you talk to yourself is the most important opinion in the world.

The moral of my story is that I had a fire in my heart for writing. It took one person to look past what I looked like, and now my passion is spreading like a wildfire.

Never put others down. We are all a generation of brilliantly talented women, so let's bring each other up. Never let someone dull your sparkle because they are unhappy with themselves.

You matter.

Sincerely,
Shania, 20, California
Student and Writer

Dear Good Girl,

Domestic violence is not something that should be taken lightly; it can be deadly. I know that many do not have the voice to speak up or the ability to escape, so maybe my story will help.

I met someone who told me he was twenty-three when I was nineteen years old. I met him at my local college's church group, and he seemed perfect. He paid for everything, took me to football games, introduced me to his friends and family—I grew to think of him as the right man for me. However, a member of the church and my parents told me to be careful and cautious of him.

After several months, I was accused of cheating on him with other men. I was not raised to behave like this, and the accusations were completely false. I lived with my parents, up the road from him, so he knew the truth. This was only the beginning of all the problems.

He called all of my friends and told them I had cheated on him, so they chose not to speak to me or accept any of my calls or texts. After the damage, the only person that was left was him, and I was afraid of losing him, too.

I believed that we'd worked things out, and at this point my parents hated him and did not want me near him. But I was already so captivated, so I ignored them. At this point, my parents decided that I could live on my own if I was to keep seeing him. They had kicked me out, and I had no one else to live with except him.

I started to learn quickly what kind of man he was. He took my cell phone and wouldn't allow me to speak to my family. I had no friends except his friends, and I was not allowed to attend church or attend anything that might give me the opportunity to speak to someone. I dropped out of college and started working. I couldn't dress nicely or wear makeup, and I could not talk to any men, except his father. His father would let me in the house every time I got off work, and his mom would try to help by buying me clothes. But all other communication was off limits.

He eventually had to give me a cell phone so that he could keep tabs on me. He made me take pictures every time I got into a vehicle, building, etc. The hitting began long before that night and would often happen on my arms, side, or legs, so that people wouldn't see the bruises.

Throughout all of this, I was able to gain enough courage to call my parents and escape within an hour. My parents showed up to the apartment with guns and ready for anything. Before my parents arrived, he threw me into the wall and ended up cutting his own hand. His parents showed up and told me that "This will be the biggest mistake of your life, leaving him … a successful businessman, of all people." I looked at him and grabbed my things. I cried for days, but I was relieved and knew I had done the right thing. Months after the breakup, he would run/jog past my parents' house where I was staying, and his parents would drive past my house often.

Although his family thought I would never be successful after leaving him, I proved them wrong. I am now married to an amazing man who accepts my story and loves me for it. I have a bachelor of science in child and family studies, with an emphasis in family relations and a minor in psychology. I am a certified family life educator and a mental health and domestic violence advocate. In December of 2017, I will receive my masters of art in professional counseling.

Don't ever let someone control or define how you should live your life. Keep your strength in the good times and bad.

Sincerely,
Danielle, 26, Mississippi
Psychologist and Domestic Violence Advocate

Dear Good Girl,

I have always been the background girl. You know, the one that people liked but never went out of their way for. I wasn't bullied; I wasn't praised; I was just me. As an adult, not much has changed, I don't have many friends. I have felt my whole life that as I achieve things people tend to pull away.

Having two small daughters, I am overjoyed to be a part of the #GoodGirlMovement. There is nothing more that I want to achieve as a mother than to have my two girls be encouragers. I want to raise kindhearted children who care for others and are not dampened by others' success. I pray every night that they have kind hearts. Every time I leave my three-year-old at pre-school, I whisper in her ear, "Be brave and be kind." She always replies, "Brave and kind."

I have always felt strongly about the quote, "Be kind to others, as you do not know the struggles they are facing." I wish that when I was younger others would have thought of me more. Nobody cared what was going on in my life, nor did they ask.

I'm sure that it was obvious that I did not have the best home life, but none of my "friends" ever asked. I always went out of my way to make sure others felt okay. I would pray that someone else would do the same for me, so that I could share my struggles. Despite the non-support, I survived, and I'm proud of that. I also do not focus on negativity, but I do focus on making sure my daughters know to be kind and genuine to others. I encourage them to be kind, not for recognition but because it is the right thing to do.

Doing the right thing is always the right thing to do.

Sincerely,
Amanda, 31, Nevada

The Good Girl Always Wins

Think like a queen. A queen is not afraid to fail. Failure is another stepping stone to greatness.
—Oprah Winfrey

This is the most important chapter. As a strong woman, you will be faced with times that challenge your faith and your self-image. As a woman who has been through a lot, I want to tell you that being yourself will always lead to success in your own respect. However, don't take my word for it. Take a look at powerful women who were written off as incompetent. They had people tell them time and time again that they were not going to be a successful ——. Now close your eyes and fill in that blank. Do you see the word *president*, *lawyer* or even *mom* appear? If you do, that is your passion. Believe it or not, we were all made to do something, and no matter what that something is, I want to encourage you to be the best at it and always stay kind. Whenever life gets rough, just remember that your break is coming.

Lucille Ball

We know her as Lucy from *I Love Lucy*, but before she landed her first big role she was considered a B-rated actress. With her passion and loving spirit, she was able to impress the right people and became one of Hollywood's most influential women of all time.

Oprah Winfrey

I think we can all agree that Oprah is the queen. In fact, she is the reason I became a journalist. At age twenty-three she was fired from her first television job in Baltimore, because she would get too attached to the stories she was covering. Now she is worth over $3 billion dollars and is considered one of the most passionate women in television.

Vera Wang

Before she was the designer, Vera Wang was a figure skater with a dream of skating at the Olympics. After she failed to make the US Olympic figure-skating team, she worked as an editor at Vogue for fifteen years and started designing her own dresses by the young age of forty. Now she is considered one of the most respected women in fashion.

J. K. Rowling

As a single mother on welfare, Rowling went to twelve different publishers and got rejected every time. She eventually sold her book for $4,000, and now she is a billionaire. Not only did she win the hearts of millions, but she also broke millions of record sales.

The point of those analogies is that you cannot kill passion and that as a good girl in society you will be fueled by passion. Each rejection brings you one step closer to your breakthrough, and no matter how old you are, you are never too old to accomplish something magical. None of those women did it for the fame or the money. They did it because they had a product that was priceless and could change the world. You also have a product. If you have learned anything from my book, it is how to be resilient in a world that is telling you that you will fail. I am cheering for you. I know that you are a good girl, and even better, an asset to the world. Do not let the world make you hard, and do not let the words of others reflect in your attitude. You are 100 percent in control of your actions.

If those women had given up, they would have spent their entire lives asking, *What if...?* Like those powerful women, you will take risks and put yourself out there because you believe in what you have to offer. There are billions of people but only one you. Be the exception; be the girl who puts others first but knows how to say no. Be strong and kind. You'll always win in the end.

How to Be the Girl You Deserve to Be

*Each time a woman stands up
for herself, without knowing
it possibly, without claiming it,
she stands up for all women.*

—MAYA ANGELOU

1. Rid yourself of toxins.

If you rid yourself of the things that steal your passion and distract you, it will provide you with a clear pathway to develop your craft. You are far more important than anyone who tells you that you do not deserve the best. I advise you to cut out meaningless activities, because they do not feed your ambition. If you are engaging in activities that spark your creativity, you'll be more apt to capitalize on those opportunities.

2. Stay focused.

As easy as it sounds, the world sometimes gets in the way. When you go off to college, there will be times when other options might look more entertaining than doing your homework, but the homework is what is going to lead to a paycheck. Put in the grunt work when you are young; that way you can enjoy the ride when you're older. Focus on the person you want to be and work your butt off so that you can become her.

3. Find your sparkle.

Don't worry, I'm not going to go Elle Woods on you. I'm simply suggesting you find something about yourself that is different and allow that to be your sparkle. For me, it was my love of talking and people. Your sparkle can be anything you want! Think of the one quality about yourself that you cannot be —— (your name) without. Without my love of people, I wouldn't be Alexis.

4. Find your energy boost!

There will be times that you feel exhausted, and your will to succeed will not be enough to motivate you. Find something that inspires you to wake up in the morning with a winning attitude. Whether it is working out, listening to music, reading, or dancing, you have to find something that allows you to connect with yourself and find your balance. At times you have to be alone to know that you can stand tall as an individual.

5. Never stop learning.

Every day I learn something new about either the world or myself. If you already know everything, you can never improve. You want to improve and become better every day. Our world is constantly evolving and we find our expectations changing weekly. Adapt to the change, and find a way to learn to excel daily. This is a really hard piece of advice, but do not be afraid to take criticism. I used to get defensive, but now I take others' advice and use it to increase my value. Learning is something that is universal; it never changes with age. You are never too old to improve.

6. Make your *own* legacy.

I grew up with two pretty successful parents, and when I was younger I used to always try to prove that I was enough just being myself. Then I realized that I didn't have to try to be something I was not. I decided that my legacy would be as a talk-show host who could connect with the audience in a profound way. You have to do the same thing—find what you want to do (even if it is the same thing as your parents), and own it. My dad always says that he wants me to be better than he ever was, and I've used that as motivation to find a craft that is completely my own. No matter what you do, please realize that you are in that position because of your own talents, not your family's. Your legacy is something only you can create.

7. Do not be afraid to fail.

If you are a perfectionist, like me, you dislike anything that re-motely resembles failure. (However, I was so thankful that my professors in college allowed me to fail, because it taught me more about myself.) At times, you're not going to be perfect, and there will be days when everything goes wrong, but you have to keep a positive outlook. Do not be afraid to fail, because that means you are at least putting yourself out there and trying. I've always been blunt; if I like a guy, I tell him. If I want a job, I tell the boss. I'm not afraid to put myself out there. As a strong woman, you will not be afraid to put yourself out there either. Step outside your comfort zone and prove yourself to the world. If you give it your all, failure will not dictate who you are.

Most importantly, love life and yourself. Happy girls are the ones who have books written about them. Your canvas is blank and waiting to be filled with color. Keep your colors bright and your imagination vivid. You were meant to be great in your own right!

Beware of Happiness Haters

It's lonely at the top.

—RANDY BLOOMER

*H*ave you ever noticed that the better you are doing, the more adversity you face? One of my friends recently said, "I don't care if I'm at the top or at the bottom. I've been in both positions, and I've always been the person that is happy to see others doing well." In this day and age, that attitude is difficult to find. Like that friend, Cindy, I've always had this attitude as well. I've often been in a position to see my friends succeed or achieve a new accolade, and I've watched as those around them begin making excuses to grow distant from them. Although I find that discouraging, I've always promised myself that I would never become like that. I would never become a happiness hater.

By definition a hater is:

(Noun)
+A person who greatly dislikes a specified person or thing.
+A negative or critical person.

I don't know about you, but I never want to be classified as that person. I've learned that by *not* hating on someone else for being successful and happy, you rid yourself of any concern. Then you can focus on bettering yourself. The best thing you can do is use the success of others as motivation.

I have nothing to complain about; life has been good to me. With hard work, I have been able to achieve everything I wanted. With that territory comes a lot of rejection from people whom I considered friends. When you reach a certain level, at any age, you'll realize that people start to question you as a person—without considering the things you might have done for them in the past. Suddenly, all the times you helped them financially, motivated them during their low points, and congratulated them during their high points becomes completely irrelevant, and you're stuck. You try to make them feel better and compensate for their loss of confidence. *Don't do that!* A good friend will never try to make you feel sorry for them because you're doing well. A good friend will celebrate you as a person and never make you question your achievements. A good friend will use your success story as motivation to create his or her own success story. Most importantly, a good person who wants more out of life will recognize your hard work and dedication and want to surround him/herself with goal-driven individuals like you.

In today's society, people are afraid to be powerful and successful. Maybe it is because they don't want the pressure of being different or the responsibility of being winners. But being different is what *makes* you successful and a winner. CEOs and influential individuals often have several associates but very few friends. Why is that? Selfish people cannot handle not being the most important person in the group! I'll let you in on a little secret. In some group, somewhere, you will be the most important person there; every person has a place where he or she belongs. But don't sacrifice relationships and friendships because you're on a different level of the success totem pole. Each step on the ladder is another step toward your end goal. Don't let the happiness haters on the steps below you dictate your future.

Work hard, because the end goal is worth it. Once you find other people who belong in your circle and who celebrate who you are, your happiness will reflect in theirs. If you see someone who has a great relationship or great job, share his or her happiness. All it does is motivate you, promotes good karma, and makes you less selfish in the long run. The world needs more of that. It needs more people with fiery passions, who illuminate happiness in their lives and in the lives of others. If we focus more on promoting happiness and success, it will encourage people to work toward having both of those things.

Never be afraid to celebrate your accomplishments; you worked for them. *Never* be a gold digger, be a goal digger. *Never* make someone feel selfish because they achieved something; your breakthrough is coming. Stay positive, and be someone worth looking up to. The world needs more of those kind of people and fewer happiness haters.

#GoodGirl Commandments

1. The good girl does not put others down to make herself look good.
2. The good girl surrounds herself with other strong good girls and does not question her beliefs to fit in.
3. The good girl smiles in the presence of other women. She knows she is an example to all those around her.
4. The good girl chooses positivity, even in the most inopportune times.
5. The good girl shows respect to those around her and respects authority, elders, and herself.
6. The good girl stands and respects our flag, because she realizes that the red, white, and blue stand for something much bigger than herself. (She also does not talk during the national anthem.)
7. The good girl respects her body and cherishes her body as her most personal attribute.
8. The good girl thinks for herself and uses her head before she makes decisions.

9. The good girl closes her ears to any drama and closes her mouth before she says anything hurtful.

10. The good girl shows kindness, even in the most competitive career field. She knows that her talent will set her apart.

11. The good girl takes care of herself and realizes that she can be her body's best friend or worst enemy.

12. The good girl is not obnoxious. She garners attention by the way she carries herself.

13. The good girl does not force a bad or unhealthy relationship.

14. The good girl does not cheat; she has strength to do the right thing.

15. The good girl does not bully—not in her relationships, friendships, family, career, or any other situation.

16. The good girl does not need a reminder to be a decent human. Her existence alone makes her want to be a better person.

Be One Hell of a Woman

Be the type of woman that
when your feet hit the floor
in the morning, the devil
says, "Oh hell, she's up!"

Congratulations, darling! You are now one hell of a woman! In this book, I've highlighted several issues that we, as women, face daily. Although people say it is hard to be a lady in this corrupt society, we are proving them wrong. We do not make excuses for the situations we are put in—we deal with them head-on.

If you are a trendsetter and believe in the power of your dreams, you can join the #GoodGirlMovement. This is not an organization in which we look down on other women or act as if we do no wrong. We admit we make mistakes, and we learn from them.

Nowadays, being a good girl has the negative connotation of being a snob, but that is not what you are. You are a woman who values her body, her mind, and her future. You live with grace and walk humbly. If you believe that you have these attributes, you are now an official member of the #GoodGirlMovement.

When you go to post on social media, remind yourself that no matter what your race, religion, or political beliefs, being a woman is a universal commonality. We are all connected through our gender, and we face a lot of the same issues. Tag us on social media, and we can create a revolution of women. Are you with me?

With us, you're never alone and you're always enough.

I'm cheering for you!

A. Bloomer

Join the Movement

Follow @goodgirlmovement
on Instagram and submit
your story today!

_____

_____

_____

_____

_____

_____

_____

_____

_____

_____

_____

_____

_____

_____

_____

About the Author

$\mathscr{A}$lexis Bloomer has emerged herself in the media industry since she was seventeen. She hosted a stage show, interviewed at red carpet events, hosted a Sirius XM radio show, interned for journalist Dan Rather, and opened her own media company, Breaking Records Media. The author of *Kindness Is Key* has shown women you can accomplish your dreams if you have the courage to do so. And it's possible while you, "Work hard, and be kind."

CPSIA information can be obtained
at www.ICGtesting.com
Printed in the USA
LVOW12s0251210118
563387LV00001B/106/P